IMAGES
of America

BOSTON
POLICE DEPARTMENT

This book is dedicated to Boston's police officers—
past, present, and future.

IMAGES
of America

BOSTON
POLICE DEPARTMENT

Donna M. Wells
Foreword by Commissioner Paul F. Evans

ARCADIA
PUBLISHING

Published by Arcadia Publishing
Charleston SC, Chicago IL, Portsmouth NH, San Francisco CA

Printed in the United States of America

Library of Congress Catalog Card Number: 2003107897

For all general information contact Arcadia Publishing at:
Telephone 843-853-2070
Fax 843-853-0044
E-mail sales@arcadiapublishing.com
For customer service and orders:
Toll-Free 1-888-313-2665

Visit us on the Internet at www.arcadiapublishing.com

Acknowledgments

I would like to thank the following people for their advice, research assistance, support, and enthusiasm for the project: the Boston Herald's Dana Bisbee, the department's director of communication Bruce Blake, James Cregg, Boston Herald librarian John Cronin, Sgt. Mary Crowley, Capt. John Dow (retired), Det. Eddie Doyle, Michael Doyle, Commissioner Paul Evans, Lisa Fehan, the department's legal advisor Mary Jo Harris, staff attorney Bill Hoch, Smith & Wesson historian Roy Jinks, George Keenan, Greg Mahoney, Sgt. Christine McKenna, president of the Boston Police Detectives Benevolent Society Det. Tom Montgomery, PO John Pugsley Jr., Clara Ruggiero of the BPD Personnel Records, Sgt. Robert Silva of the department's identification and photograph unit, PO John Slattery of the Boston Police Relief Association, Sgt. Det. Herb Spellman (retired) of the department's homicide unit, Superintendent in Chief William J. Taylor (retired), James P. Teed, and William Werner.

Special thanks go to my parents, Edward and Jane Wells, my husband, Jeffrey Kelley, and my friend Julie Robinson for not having any doubts, even if I did.

A thank-you also goes to Abby for keeping me company.

CONTENTS

FOREWORD

Boston is a city that enjoys celebrating its rich heritage. This is perhaps unsurprising, given its long and colorful history. Somewhat less well known, however, is the fact that the Boston Police Department has played an interesting and often important role in much of this history.

Back in 1630, when John Winthrop offered his famously idealized description of Boston as a shining "City Upon a Hill," he knew that in reality it was still little more than a simple, Colonial fishing village. However, in what was perhaps a hint of the town fathers' future hopes and aspirations, they quickly decided to organize a corps of watchmen to guard themselves and their neighbors from harm. This small, unpaid band of protectors was the genesis of what would one day become the Boston Police Department. As our nation's oldest, it remains the focal point for a proud tradition of public service to this day.

After being constituted in a number of forms, the department was officially created in 1854. Then as now, the job was often difficult and dangerous, as the names of those listed on our Roll of Honor sadly illustrate. In time, advances such as telephones, radio equipment, automobiles, and computer technology revolutionized the provision of police services, both in Boston and beyond. Meanwhile, the city itself grew to become a vibrant collection of bustling neighborhoods that people from around the world now call home.

A long list of intellectual, political, and cultural leaders have worked over the course of many decades to build and shape the modern city of Boston that we know today. A similarly industrious group of men and women have worked along with them, often behind the scenes, to keep the peace and ensure the public's safety and well being as members of the Boston Police Department. This book is a celebration of their important legacy. I hope you will enjoy it.

—Police Commissioner Paul F. Evans
Boston, Massachusetts, 2003

INTRODUCTION

The nation's oldest police department, the Boston Police Department, celebrates its formal 150th anniversary in 2004, but the department traces its origins to the establishment of the Night Watch with an officer and six men in 1631. That organization functioned more along the lines of a military guard, but by 1635, the Night Watch consisted of property-owning male citizens over the age of 16 who were required to take the duty by turn. They were unpaid until 1703, when the pay was set at 35 shillings a month.

In 1749, written rules were first drafted for the government of the Watch. In 1796, the Watch was reorganized and the watchmen carried a badge of office, a hook with a bill, and the rattle, a noise-making devise used for calling for assistance.

On December 12, 1825, Watchman Jonathan Houghton became the first Boston law-enforcement officer killed in the line of duty. He was killed on State Street by John Halloran, who was hung for the crime in March 1826. Watchman Houghton's name, along with that of David Estes, who was killed in 1848, was recently sponsored by the department for inclusion on the National Law Enforcement Memorial in Washington, D.C., and the inclusion was approved in 2002.

In 1838, the Day Police was organized, having no connection with the Night Watch. It operated under the city marshal, and six officers were appointed. In 1846, the force was reorganized, with 22 officers on the day shift and 8 night officers.

In 1852, the office of city marshal was abolished, and the office of chief of police was created. Francis Tukey, who had been the marshal, was appointed the first chief of police.

In 1853, the Harbor Police was created in response to the increase in robberies of occupied vessels in the waters of Boston Harbor. The policemen were furnished with rowboats and armed with Colt revolvers. This was the first unit furnished with firearms.

In May 1854, the Boston Night Watch and Day Police were disbanded, and the Boston Police Department came into being. Robert Taylor was appointed chief of police. On the very first evening of the reorganization, the entire force was called out to suppress the riot caused by the arrest of the fugitive slave Anthony Burns. The old hook and bill, which had been in use for 154 years, was replaced by a 14-inch club. The central office was located in the old courthouse in Court Square. There were eight station houses, located at the following locations: the old Hancock School at 209 Hanover Street in the North End; 21 Court Square at Williams Court; Leverett Street in the West End; the rear of Boylston Market at the Washington Street and Boylston Street intersection; Canton Street Place in the South End; 194 West Broadway in

South Boston; Paris Street in East Boston; and Lincoln's Wharf (the Harbor Police).

In 1858, Boston officers put on uniforms for the first time. The chief wore a blue dress coat with tails, black pants, a buff merino vest, and a black top hat with a gold star in a rosette on the hat. The deputy chief wore a blue frock coat, blue or black pants, a light buff vest, and a black top hat with a gold star or enameled leather. Captains wore blue dress coats with tails, buff marseilles vests, black pants, and black top hats. Lieutenants and patrolmen wore double-breasted, dark-blue frock coats, dark-blue pants, and black silk, satin, or cotton vests, depending on the season. Lieutenants wore black top hats, and patrolmen wore black billed caps.

Barney McGinniskin was the first Irishman appointed to the force c. 1862. He was assigned to Division 4, but Marshal Tukey refused to assign him street duty. McGinniskin worked inside the station for about three years before Tukey fired him.

In 1863, the officers were supplied with 24-inch clubs. At this time, the officers did not officially carry firearms.

In 1865, upon the completion of the new city hall, the central office moved there from the old courthouse in Court Square.

In 1871, the central office was connected to all the station houses by telegraph. Prior to this, the only communication method was by messenger.

At approximately 7:30 p.m. on November 9, 1872, the Great Boston Fire started. It was reportedly discovered by a Patrolman Page of Division 4, who was chasing some boys on Lincoln Street. He saw fire at a building at 83–85 Summer Street and gave an alarm at Box 52 at Bedford and Lincoln Streets. The entire force was called out to prevent looting and maintain order. The fire covered about 60 acres, destroying property valued at $100 million, including approximately 1,500 places of business.

In 1873, one mounted officer was assigned to patrol Mill Dam Road, the present-day Beacon Street. This was so successful that by 1874, there were 28 mounted officers on duty in the city. In 1874, the *Protector*, the department's first steam-powered vessel, was put into service, the department's sailboat having been sold in 1870.

In 1875, station houses began distributing free soup to the poor and distributed turkeys for Thanksgiving, activities that continued, with occasional pauses, until 1888. At this time, station houses had been offering simple lodging to indigent people since at least 1858.

In 1878, the office of chief of police was abolished and the Board of Police Commissioners was created. There were three commissioners who were appointed by the mayor. The superintendent of police was the executive officer. Also, in 1878, the first telephones were installed in the department.

In his book, *Boston Events*, Edward Savage records that in 1879, the first "colored" officer was appointed. Sadly, he did not record the individual's name, and it remains unknown. The first documented African-American Boston police officer was Harvey B. Yates, who was hired after the strike in October 1919. He served until 1956.

In 1883, the central office moved into new quarters at Pemberton Square. A new steam launch, named *Patrol*, was also put into service.

In 1884, the city council voted to provide the officers with firearms. Seven hundred Smith & Wesson .38 double-action-break-open-automatic-ejector-style revolvers were purchased at a cost of $9 each and distributed to the officers. The guns had 3.25-inch barrels with black hard-rubber grips marked "BPD" on the back.

In 1885, the power to appoint the Board of Police Commissioners was transferred from the mayor to the governor.

In 1886, after approximately five years of trials at various divisions, all of the divisions were equipped with signal boxes by the Municipal Signal Company. These signal boxes allowed patrol officers to contact the station houses.

In 1887, matrons were appointed at station houses, under the Acts of 1887, chapter 234, which provided for the appointment of police matrons in cities and established a house of detention for women in the city of Boston. These were the first women employed in a law-enforcement capacity by the department. They had no powers of arrest, but served as guards for women and juvenile prisoners.

In 1896, four park police were equipped with bicycles, beginning a long tradition of Boston officers on two wheels. The new harbor patrol vessel, the *Guardian,* was commissioned.

A new uniform was introduced *c.* 1900. It consisted of high-necked frock coats, above which protruded a winged collar, and a polished leather belt with a buckle bearing the city seal. The officers wore high domed helmets, grey in the summer and navy blue in the winter.

In 1903, the nation's first motor patrol was established in Boston. A Stanley Steamer automobile was purchased. Driven by a civilian chauffeur, the officer sat on a higher seat so that he could look over the high backyard fences in the Back Bay. By 1906, the department owned five automobiles, four one-seaters, and a larger vehicle for department officials. In 1912, the first patrol wagon was put into service in Division 17, West Roxbury.

In 1906, the Board of Police Commissioners was abolished. There was now a single commissioner appointed by the governor.

In 1919, Boston's police officers had formed a social club, since forming a union was forbidden by department rules. Unhappy with their pay and general working conditions, the members of the social club petitioned the department for a raise. Rebuffed, they joined the American Federation of Labor, becoming the Boston Police Union, No. 16,807. Commissioner Edwin Curtis dismissed John F. McInnes, the president of the union, and 18 other union leaders. In response, on September 9, 1919, over 1,100 of the department's 1,500 officers went on strike. Those officers were judged by the commissioner as having abandoned their duty and were dismissed. They were never reinstated. In order to protect the city, volunteer police officers were recruited, the Metropolitan Police were called to duty and, eventually, the Massachusetts State Guard was called in to restore order. After the strike, the newly hired officers received all the benefits the strikers had sought to gain, with the exception of the right to form a union.

In 1920, a new uniform was introduced. A short tunic coat replaced the long frock coats and a military-type billed cap was adopted. In 1921, the department hired its first female police officers. They worked with women and juveniles and did not have powers of arrest. In 1926, a new headquarters building at 154 Berkeley Street was occupied.

In 1931, the first Boston police school was established. There was a one-way radio system in service by 1934, as cars were equipped with receivers only. All dispatching was done from headquarters. By 1936, cars were equipped with receivers and transmitters. The signal service system was retained until 1968.

In 1943, the Crime Prevention Bureau was created. The main objective of the bureau was to "meet the pressing problems of juvenile delinquency." The women who were hired in 1921 were transferred to this bureau and given powers of arrest. In 1948, Margaret McHugh became the department's first female detective. She retired in 1959.

In 1962, the tactical patrol force was established in response to student and racial unrest and to respond to unusual or sudden emergencies. The power to appoint the police commissioner was transferred back to the mayor. In 1963, patrol divisions were changed to patrol districts.

In 1964, the K-9 unit was created. This unit began with six dogs donated by German reporters grateful for the cooperation they had received from Boston officers in their coverage of the Boston Strangler murders. They also paid for the chief dog trainer of the Berlin Police Department to teach Boston's officers how to work with the dogs. In 1965, the Boston Police Patrolmen's Association was founded. In 1998, they received the American Federation of Labor charter No. 16,807, the very one that was issued to the social club of 1919. Superior officers and detectives each later formed separate unions.

In 1972, an improved radio system was installed, along with the 911 emergency reporting system. Also, in 1972, the Boston Police Academy began admitting women. In 1974, with the advent of court-ordered school busing, the mobile operations patrol was created. The squad was composed of officers on motorcycles, able to respond quickly to disturbances and restore order.

In 1997, the department moved into its new, state-of-the-art headquarters, named in memory of brothers Walter and John Schroeder. Both Boston officers were killed in the line of duty.

In 1998, the department's crime lab became the first nationally accredited public forensic DNA analysis laboratory in New England.

Today's Boston Police Department is very different from that of even 20 years ago. Officers use advanced forensic, identification, and communication technologies. But the mission of the Boston Police Department is the same as it was in those very early days, when officers carried only lanterns and hooks and called the hours. In 2004, the Boston Police Department dedicates itself to working in partnership with the community to fight crime, reduce fear, and improve the quality of life in Boston neighborhoods. Its continuing mission is neighborhood policing.

One

PEOPLE

THE PUGSLEY CLAN. This photograph was taken on the occasion of the appointment of the fifth son of the Arthur Pugsley family in 1959. From left to right are Ernest, Arthur Jr., Arthur Sr., Charles, Robert, and Stanley Pugsley. In 1963, the sixth and seventh sons, John and Richard, joined the force. John Jr., grandson of Arthur and son of John, was appointed on June 25, 1997. (Courtesy Boston Police Department Archives.)

EDWARD HARTWELL SAVAGE. Savage was appointed to the force in 1851. In 1854, he was captain at Station 1. By 1861, he was deputy chief and in 1870, was appointed chief of police, an office that he held until 1878. His accomplishments included establishing the "Rogues' Gallery," a collection of photographs and descriptions of the physical characteristics, modus operandi, and associates of known criminals, and a descriptive system for criminal identification. During his tenure, police stations established soup kitchens and homeless shelters, and eventually, even provided shoes and medicines. (Author's collection.)

BENJAMIN P. ELDRIDGE,
c. 1897. Eldridge was appointed
a patrolman in September 1875.
He rose through the ranks and
was named superintendent of
police in November 1891. In
1897, he and Chief Inspector
William B. Watts wrote a book
together entitled *Our Rival, the
Rascal—A Faithful Portrayal of
the Conflict Between the Criminals
of this Age and the Defenders of
Society—The Police*. He retired in
1901. (Author's collection.)

WILLIAM B. WATTS, c. 1897. Watts
was appointed in December 1877 and
rose to the rank of chief inspector. He
retired in 1912. In 1899, he pursued the
Italian murderer Antonio di Blasi to
Italy and presented such evidence to the
Italian courts that di Blasi was convicted
and sentenced to prison. Watts's father,
William M. Watts, also a Boston
patrolman, served from 1860 to 1891.
(Author's collection.)

13

AN ILLUSTRATION FROM AN 1897 CHILDREN'S BOOK. The book *The King of the Park*, in which this illustration appears, was inscribed to "Police-Sergeant Charles Wesley Hebard of the Back Bay Fens." In the illustration, one of the main characters in the book, Sgt. Stephen Hardy, is depicted saving a boy from drowning. Strangely, in 1898, Sergeant Hebard saved two boys from drowning in the waters of the Back Bay Fens and was commended for the heroic act. (Author's collection.)

JOHN J. DOYLE, C. 1905. Doyle was appointed in 1905 and was one of the officers who went on strike in 1919 for improvements in wages and working conditions. He was dismissed for this act, along with approximately 1,100 of his fellow officers. His son, George F. Doyle, was appointed in 1947. George's sons, Richard and Edward, were appointed in 1966 and 1968, respectively. They both retired in 2003. (Courtesy Doyle family.)

PATROLMAN JOHN J. DOYLE. In this January 1908 photograph, Doyle is on traffic duty in front of headquarters at Pemberton Square for the funeral of fellow officer, Patrolman John J. Lynch. On January 16, 1908, at the corner of Summer and Kingston Streets, Lynch was shot by a man he was searching, and Doyle, who had just left Lynch, ran back when he heard the shots and was able to apprehend the suspect. (Courtesy Doyle family.)

PATROLMAN MARTIN J. LYONS, C. 1919. Lyons was born in Ireland in 1888. He was appointed on December 6, 1919. He spent his entire career at Division 9, retired in 1942, and died in 1961. (Courtesy Dennis Lyons.)

PATROLMAN JOSEPH J. CULPIN, C. 1923. Patrolman Culpin is wearing the new badge and uniform put into use after the strike. Gone were the Keystone Kops helmets and the long, bulky frock coat. The new uniform, with its short tunic and handsome cap, was trimmer and more modern. (Courtesy Boston Police Department Archives.)

SUPERINTENDENT MICHAEL H. CROWLEY, C. 1923.
Crowley was appointed in 1888, rose to the rank of superintendent, and died in 1933. In 1937, a new 60-foot diesel-driven police boat was named after him. (Courtesy Boston Police Department Archives.)

CAPT. THOMAS S.J. KAVANAGH, C. 1937. Kavanagh was appointed in 1908, retired in 1946 at the rank of deputy superintendent, and died in 1970. In 1937, he wrote a book entitled *Minute Police Talks: A Complete Police Manual,* in which he wrote, "Like the soldier who bears arms in defense of his country, so it is a solemn honor when you don the uniform of a policeman to protect and safeguard the public whom you serve." (Courtesy Boston Police Department Archives.)

17

THE BOSTON POLICE DEPARTMENT CLASS OF JANUARY 1941. The sign behind the new officers reads, "Our Square Deal Code, 1. No compromise with crime, 2. To be relentless toward the criminal, 3. In our judgment be charitable toward minor offenders, 4. Never to arrest if a summons will suffice, 5. Never to summons if a warning would be better, 6. Never to scold or

reprimand [if one] can inform and request, Our Motto—Courtesy and Efficiency." (Courtesy Doyle family.)

PATROLMAN GEORGE F. DOYLE, AFTER 1960. Doyle was appointed in November 1941 and retired in July 1971. He was the son of Patrolman John J. Doyle and the father of Sgt. Richard Doyle and Det. Edward Doyle. (Courtesy Doyle family.)

PATROLMAN FRANCIS E. BAILEY IN SEPTEMBER 1943. Appointed in September 1943, Bailey received several commendations before he retired in 1974. Patrolman Bailey was one of the hundreds of highly skilled Boston police officers who served their country during World War II by remaining at their posts with the department. The Boston Police Department Archives possesses his work diaries from 1943 to 1945. (Courtesy Boston Police Department Archives.)

PATROLMEN THOMAS H. SCOTT AND MICHAEL A. BOCCUZZI IN 1963. These officers received the department Medal of Honor and the Thomas F. Sullivan Award for arresting three men at gunpoint, one of whom was armed with a fully loaded automatic pistol. The suspects had robbed a market in Jamaica Plain and were still in possession of the proceeds from the robbery. The suspects were convicted and served sentences at Walpole State Prison. (Courtesy Boston Police Department Archives.)

EQUIPMENT BELONGING TO PATROLMAN EDWIN W. STEWART. This patrolman was shot in the chest by an armed-robbery suspect in Roxbury in December 1963. Patrolman Stewart recovered fully from his injuries and was part of the team of officers that arrested his assailant on July 11, 1964, on charges of attempted murder, assault and battery with a dangerous weapon, and carrying a firearm without being licensed. (Courtesy Boston Police Department Archives.)

FATHERS AND SONS. In this June 20, 1966, photograph are, from left to right, Patrolman William O'Reilly and his stepfather, Supt. Edward Connolly; Patrolman Richard Doyle and his father, Patrolman George Doyle; and Patrolman Robert Hayden Jr. and his father, Det. Robert Hayden Sr. (Courtesy Doyle Family.)

A PUGSLEY TRADITION. The Pugsley sons salute their father on the steps of headquarters at 154 Berkeley Street *c.* 1963. From left to right are Arthur Sr. (in plainclothes), Arthur Jr., Stanley, Ernest, Robert, Charles, John, and Richard. (Courtesy PO John J. Pugsley Jr.)

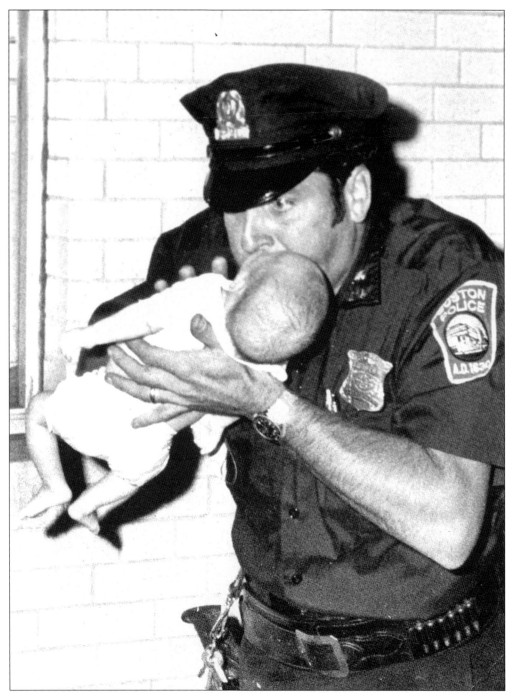

PATROLMAN EDWARD DOYLE AND STACY ANN DEWOLFE IN AUGUST 1970. Patrolman Edward Doyle is attempting to revive Stacy Ann DeWolfe. Despite attempts by Patrolman Doyle and fellow officers Thomas Kenneally and Robert Fitzgerald, the baby died. The death was later ruled of natural causes. The photograph won four awards for *Boston Record American* photographer Roland Oxton. (Courtesy Boston Herald.)

CAPT. WILLIAM J. HOGAN, C. 1972. Captain Hogan is in a setting that is familiar to every Boston police officer—a Boston Police Academy classroom. Hogan was appointed in August 1937. He was awarded the department Medal of Honor in 1947. In 1976, he was made the commander of the academy, a post he held until his retirement in 1981. In 1985, the Boston Police Academy building was named after him. (Courtesy Boston Police Department Archives.)

"HOGAN'S HEROINES." This clock hung on the wall at the academy in 1972, the first year that women were trained there as Boston police officers. The female officers represented are, clockwise starting at 12:00, Kathy Anderson, Kathy Fitzpatrick, Diane Hofferty, Sheila Kaplan, Mary Crowley, Lynn Kohansky, Pat McMaster, Chris Michaelosky, Patricia Rehm, Barbara Ridlon, Katie Thornton, and Beverly Veseleny. (Courtesy Boston Police Department Archives.)

PATROLMAN JOHN J. DOW, c. 1949. Dow was shot during World War II and lost portions of several fingers. On his return to the United States, Dow applied to the Boston Police Department but was rejected because of his disability. Dow appealed the decision, and with the support of the Civil Service Commission was appointed in 1949. He received the department Medal of Honor in 1965 and retired in 1982 at the rank of captain. (Courtesy Boston Police Department Archives.)

OFFICERS AT THE NATIONAL LAW ENFORCEMENT MEMORIAL, c. 1997. Boston officers present included Mary Crowley, Robin Demarco, Rachel Keefe, Cecelia Fagan, Maura Flynn, Lisa Lehane, and Peggy Waggett. (Courtesy Sgt. Mary Crowley.)

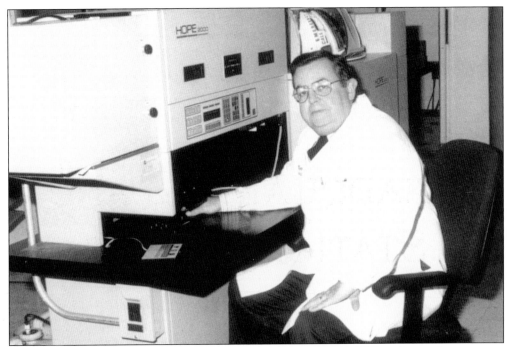

PATROLMAN DANIEL DURAN IN 1995. Duran was appointed in 1970 and spent his career in the identification and photograph unit as a police photographer and fingerprint and evidence technician. He retired in 2002. Officer Duran is seen sitting in front of a photograph printer and processor. (Courtesy Boston Police Department Archives.)

DEPUTY SUPERINTENDENT FLORASTINE CREED IN 2003. Creed was the first black woman to make the rank of sergeant detective in 1988, the first to be appointed deputy superintendent in 1994, the first to make the rank of lieutenant in 1995, and the first to be appointed superintendent in 1998. Currently, she is the department's highest ranking woman. (Courtesy Boston Police Department Archives.)

Two

HEADQUARTERS AND STATION HOUSES

BOSTON POLICE HEADQUARTERS AT ONE SCHROEDER PLAZA. Dedicated in 1997, this new facility is located in Roxbury. Etched into the granite walls of the building are the names of the 69 officers who have fallen in the line of duty since 1854. Among them are the names of brothers Walter and John Schroeder. (Courtesy Boston Police Department Archives.)

BOSTON CITY HALL. Upon completion of the city hall in 1865, police headquarters, then known as the central office, moved here from its first location, the old courthouse in Court Square. (Author's collection.)

BOSTON POLICE HEADQUARTERS AT PEMBERTON SQUARE, C. 1901. Headquarters moved here in 1883 from city hall and remained here until the completion of a new headquarters building at 154 Berkeley Street in 1926. This square was nicely appointed, having a small park in the center and a general appearance similar to Louisburg Square on Beacon Hill. (Courtesy Capt. John V. Dow (retired).)

WILLIAM H. PIERCE'S OFFICE. Seen here is the superintendent's office at the Pemberton Square headquarters *c.* 1901. (Courtesy Boston Police Department Archives.)

BYRON F. BRAGDON AND JAMES M. COULTER'S OFFICE. The office of Bragdon and Coulter, deputy superintendents, is seen in this *c.* 1901 photograph, taken at the headquarters at Pemberton Square. (Courtesy Boston Police Department Archives.)

WATTS AND DUGAN. Seen here are Chief Inspector William B. Watts and Assistant Chief Inspector Capt. Joseph Dugan *c.* 1901. (Courtesy Boston Police Department Archives.)

WATTS'S OFFICE. This is the office of Chief Inspector Watts at the Pemberton Square headquarters *c.* 1901. (Courtesy Boston Police Department Archives.)

DIVISION 1, 209 HANOVER STREET, C. 1901. This building was in use for watch and police purposes from 1849 until 1933, when the division moved to new premises on North Street. (Courtesy Boston Police Department Archives.)

THE FRONT DESK, DIVISION 1. This *c.* 1901 photograph is an interior view of Division 1 at 209 Hanover Street. (Courtesy Boston Police Department Archives.)

DIVISION 2, 21 COURT SQUARE AT WILLIAMS COURT. This station was in continuous watch and police use from 1846 to 1925, when the division moved to 229 Milk Street. In 1966, the district moved to 203 Atlantic Avenue, and it moved to its present location, 135 Dudley Street in Roxbury, in 1971. (Courtesy Boston Police Department Archives.)

THE FRONT DESK, DIVISION 2. This photograph shows the front desk of Division 2 at 21 Court Square at Williams Court c. 1901. (Courtesy Boston Police Department Archives.)

DIVISION 3, 80 JOY STREET, BEACON HILL, C. 1901. The station moved here in 1861 from Leverett Street in the West End. In 1933, the division was closed. The district reopened in 1937, operating out of its old station on Joy Street. In 1988, after having been closed again and then moved again, the district moved to its present location at 1165 Blue Hill Avenue. (Courtesy Boston Police Department Archives.)

DIVISION 4, 56 LAGRANGE STREET, NEAR TREMONT STREET, C. 1901. The division moved here from premises at the rear of Boylston Market on Washington Street. In 1933, the division moved to a new station at 7 Warren Avenue. The district moved to its present location at 650 Harrison Avenue in 2001. (Courtesy Boston Police Department Archives.)

THE FRONT DESK, DIVISION 4. This interior view of the front desk of Division 4 was taken *c.* 1901, when the station was located on Lagrange Street. (Courtesy Boston Police Department Archives.)

DIVISION 5, 21 EAST DEDHAM STREET, C. 1901. The station moved here, the corner of East Dedham and Mystic Streets in the South End, from Canton Street Place in the South End. In 1933, Division 5 was closed and its territory incorporated into Division 4. In 1964, District 5 was reestablished at 1249 Hyde Park Avenue in Hyde Park. In 1979, a new District 5 station was built at 1708 Centre Street in West Roxbury. (Courtesy Boston Police Department Archives.)

THE FRONT DESK, DISTRICT 5. Seen here is the District 5 front desk at the 21 East Dedham Street location *c.* 1901. (Courtesy Boston Police Department Archives.)

DIVISION 6, 194 WEST BROADWAY, c. 1901. Division 6 occupied this West Broadway location, near C Street in South Boston, from *c.* 1854 until 1915. It then moved to 273 D Street in South Boston. Division 6 was closed at the D Street location in 1981 and reopened at its present location, 101 West Broadway in 1989. (Courtesy Boston Police Department Archives.)

THE FRONT DESK, DISTRICT 6. Seen here is an interior view of District 6 at its West Broadway location *c.* 1901. (Courtesy Boston Police Department Archives.)

DIVISION 7, 50 MERIDIAN STREET, EAST BOSTON, THE FRONT DESK, C. 1901. The station moved here from Paris Street, East Boston, in 1859. In 1913, a new station was constructed at 69 Paris Street, the district's current location. (Courtesy Boston Police Department Archives.)

Division 8, Commercial and Battery Streets, the North End, c. 1901. The Harbor Patrol unit was established in 1853 to combat the many robberies that were being committed on vessels in Boston Harbor. The station moved here from Lincoln's Wharf in 1866. In 1923, a new station at 521 Commercial Street was occupied. The station closed in 1973. In 1980, Harbor Patrol was reestablished and continues today. (Courtesy Boston Police Department Archives.)

The Front Desk, Division 8. Seen here is the front desk of Division 8, located at Commercial and Battery Streets *c.* 1901. (Courtesy Boston Police Department Archives.)

DIVISION 9, 409 DUDLEY STREET, ROXBURY, C. 1901. Division 9 was established with the annexation of Roxbury to Boston in 1868. In 1872, the station moved here, to the corner of Dudley Street and Mount Pleasant Avenue, from the basement of Roxbury's city hall at Dudley and Putnam Streets. In 1971, Districts 9 and 10 were consolidated into District 2, with a new station at 135 Dudley Street. (Courtesy Boston Police Department Archives.)

DIVISION 10, 1170 COLUMBUS AVENUE, ROXBURY CROSSING, THE FRONT DESK, C. 1901.
This interior view shows the front desk of Division 10, located at 1170 Columbus Avenue in
Roxbury Crossing. (Courtesy Boston Police Department Archives.)

DIVISION 11, FIELDS CORNER, DORCHESTER, C. 1901. This division was located at 195 Adams Street, on the corner of Arcadia Street. Established with the annexation of Dorchester in 1870, District 11 was first housed at Kane Square. Four substations were established by 1874. The division moved here in 1875. The substations closed when Division 19 opened at 872 Morton Street in Mattapan. District C-11 moved to its current location at 40 Gibson Street in Dorchester in 1971. (Courtesy Boston Police Department Archives.)

THE FRONT DESK, DIVISION 11. Seen here is a *c.* 1901 interior view of the Division 11 station. (Courtesy Boston Police Department Archives.)

DIVISION 12, EAST 4TH STREET, NEAR K STREET, SOUTH BOSTON, C. 1901. The division was established at this location in 1874 and remained here until 1933, when Divisions 6 and 12 were consolidated into a new Division 6. The new division operated out of the existing old Division 6 station house at 273 D Street, South Boston. (Courtesy Boston Police Department Archives.)

THE FRONT DESK, DIVISION 12. An interior view of the East 4th Street station of Division 12 is seen in this c. 1901 photograph. (Courtesy Boston Police Department Archives.)

DIVISION 13, 28 SEAVERNS AVENUE, JAMAICA PLAIN, C. 1901. This division was established in 1874, with the annexation of West Roxbury. The division remained in this location until the late 1980s, when the station house was sold and converted to condominiums and District E-13 moved to a new station at 3345 Washington Street, Jamaica Plain. (Courtesy Boston Police Department Archives.)

THE FRONT DESK, DIVISION 13. Seen here is the Division 13 interior *c.* 1901. (Courtesy Boston Police Department Archives.)

DIVISION 14, 301 WASHINGTON STREET, BRIGHTON, C. 1901. This division was established in 1874, with the annexation of Brighton. The first station was located in Brighton's town hall on Washington Street. The division moved to a new station house at 301 Washington Street in 1893 and has remained at this location until the present day. The building is the oldest continuously occupied station house in the city. (Courtesy Boston Police Department Archives.)

THE FRONT DESK, DIVISION 14. Seen in this *c.* 1901 view is the front desk of Division 14, located at 301 Washington Street in Brighton. (Courtesy Boston Police Department Archives.)

DIVISION 15, CHARLESTOWN CITY HALL, CITY SQUARE, c. 1901. This division was established in 1874, with the annexation of Charlestown. The division remained in this location until 1914, when a new station at 3 City Square in Charlestown was occupied. In 1981, Division 15 was closed, and its territory was incorporated into District A-1. (Courtesy Boston Police Department Archives.)

THE FRONT DESK, DIVISION 15. In this interior view is the Division 15 front desk *c.* 1901. (Courtesy Boston Police Department Archives.)

DIVISION 16, 951 BOYLSTON STREET, NEAR HEREFORD STREET, BACK BAY, C. 1901. This division was established in 1888 and remained at this location until 1964, when it was closed and its territory was incorporated into District D-4. (Courtesy Boston Police Department Archives.)

THE FRONT DESK, DIVISION 16. The Division 16 station interior is seen in this c. 1901 view. (Courtesy Boston Police Department Archives.)

DISTRICT A-1, 40 SUDBURY STREET, GOVERNMENT CENTER. This late 1960s photograph shows the District A-1 building, occupied from 1968 to today. (Courtesy Boston Police Department Archives.)

DISTRICT 2, 203 ATLANTIC AVENUE. The building seen in this 1960s photograph was occupied by District 2 from 1966 until 1971. (Courtesy Boston Police Department Archives.)

DISTRICT B-2, 135 DUDLEY STREET, ROXBURY, 1995. This building has served as the District B-2 station from 1971 to today. (Courtesy Boston Police Department Archives.)

DISTRICT 3, 872 MORTON STREET, MATTAPAN. This station served as headquarters for Division 19 from 1915 until 1964, when it was occupied as District 3 until 1988. (Courtesy Boston Police Department Archives.)

DISTRICT 6, 273 D STREET, SOUTH BOSTON. The building seen in this 1960s photograph was occupied from 1915 to 1981 by District 6. (Courtesy Boston Police Department Archives.)

DISTRICT C-6, 101 WEST BROADWAY, 1995. This District C-6 building on West Broadway has been occupied since 1989. (Courtesy Boston Police Department Archives.)

DISTRICT A-7, 69 PARIS STREET, EAST BOSTON, 1995. This building was occupied from 1913 to present. (Courtesy Boston Police Department Archives.)

DIVISION 8, 521 COMMERCIAL STREET. Seen in this 1960s photograph, the Harbor Patrol station was occupied from 1923 to 1973. (Courtesy Boston Police Department Archives.)

THE DIVISION 8 DOCK. Seen is the patrol boat *Protector* at dock in the 1960s. (Courtesy Boston Police Department Archives.)

DISTRICT C-11, 40 GIBSON STREET, DORCHESTER, 1995. This district building has been occupied since 1971. (Courtesy Boston Police Department Archives.)

THE OFFICERS OF DIVISION 15. Seen at the city hall in Charlestown are the officers of Division 15. This photograph was taken after 1874. (Courtesy Boston Police Department Archives.)

DIVISION 15, 3 CITY SQUARE, CHARLESTOWN, C. THE 1960S. Division 15 occupied this building from 1914 until 1981. (Courtesy Boston Police Department Archives.)

DIVISION 17, 1893 CENTRE STREET, WEST ROXBURY, 1914. The first motor patrol wagon was placed into service at this station, located at the intersection of Centre and Hastings Streets in West Roxbury, in 1912, when the division was established. In 1964, this division was closed, and its territory was incorporated into a new District 5, with headquarters at the District 18 station house at 1249 Hyde Park Avenue in Hyde Park. (Courtesy Boston Police Department Archives.)

DIVISION 18, 1249 HYDE PARK AVENUE, HYDE PARK. This division was established at 1243 Hyde Park Avenue, opposite Winthrop Street, in 1912, with the annexation of Hyde Park. In 1925, a new station was constructed at 1249 Hyde Park Avenue, the present location of District E-18. (Courtesy Boston Police Department Archives.)

HEADQUARTERS, 154 BERKELEY STREET, C. THE 1960S. Dedicated in 1926, 154 Berkeley was witness to some of the most famous Boston crimes—the Brink's robbery, the Boston Strangler crimes, and the Stuart murder. The building served the department well until 1997, when the new headquarters at One Schroeder Plaza was occupied. (Courtesy Boston Police Department Archives.)

Three

POLICE TECHNOLOGY, VEHICLES, UNIFORMS, AND EQUIPMENT

THE UNIFORMS OF 1858. The chief wore a blue dress coat, black pants, a beige merino vest, and a black silk hat with a gold star in a rosette. The deputy chief wore a blue frock coat, blue or black pants, a light beige vest, and a black silk hat with a gold star or enameled leather. Captains wore a blue dress coat, a beige marseilles vest, black pants, and a black silk hat. Lieutenants and patrolmen wore double-breasted dark blue frock coats, dark blue pants, and black silk or satin vests in the spring or autumn or black cloth vests, single breasted, in the winter. (Courtesy Boston Police Department Archives.)

THE BADGE INTRODUCED IN 1853. The 1853 badge was made of brass. In 1854, when the Boston Police Department was created from the amalgamation of the Day Police and the Night Watch, this badge was retired and replaced with a silver octagon-shaped badge, a little larger than a silver dollar, with the words "Boston Police" engraved around a five-pointed star within the octagon. (Author's collection.)

BOSTON POLICE DEPARTMENT BADGES, 1879 TO PRESENT. The badge on the left was introduced in 1879 and is known as the radiator badge due to its resemblance to the radiators of early automobiles. The badge in the center (the badge number appears on the back) was introduced in 1920, after the strike. The radiator shape was retained and the city seal, a sunburst, and an arm holding a sword were added. The shield-shaped badge on the right, introduced in 1960, is the department's current issue. (Courtesy Kellscraft Studio.)

BOSTON'S "FINEST" are Supplied with the World - Renowned

SMITH & WESSON

A Revolver that is good enough for the Boston Police should be good enough for anybody. A **cheap** revolver is a dangerous thing and unreliable for self-defense. If you have a revolver at all, have the best.

TO=DAY, while you think of it, is the time to get it.
See Your Dealer.

Catalogue of Latest Models for a Stamp.

SMITH & WESSON, 19 Stockbridge St., Springfield, Mass.

AN 1885 SMITH & WESSON ADVERTISEMENT. Smith & Wesson, proud of the fact that they had supplied the Boston Police Department with its weapons, issued this advertisement *c.* 1885. (Courtesy Smith & Wesson Archives.)

A Division 16 Patrol Wagon, after 1888. These vehicles were colloquially known as Black Marias, or paddy wagons. According to the *Oxford Dictionary of Word Histories*, "Black Maria" was a black woman named Maria Lee who ran a boardinghouse in 19th-century Boston and "helped police escort drunk and disorderly customers to jail." It is unclear whether the term "paddy" was a reference to the prisoners or the officers. (Courtesy Boston Police Department Relief Association.)

A Division 14 Patrol Wagon. This *c.* 1901 photograph shows a Division 14 patrol wagon. (Courtesy Boston Police Department Archives.)

A STANLEY STEAMER, 1903. Boston established the first motor patrol in the United States in 1903 with the purchase of a Stanley Steamer. Boston's Back Bay neighborhood had many houses with high fences in the backyards. A civilian chauffeur drove the vehicle while a police officer rode on a seat high enough to see over the fences. They covered about 60 miles a day. (Courtesy Boston Police Department Archives.)

PATROLMAN THOMAS E. BARRON. In this early 1930s photograph is Patrolman Barron (second from the left) of Division 2, located downtown, and three fellow officers who are unidentified. These early cruisers carried two officers, were not equipped with radios, and were dispatched from their stations. On August 1, 1934, patrol cars were equipped with receiving radios only. On October 1, 1936, a two-way system was installed, and all patrol cars were equipped with receivers and transmitters. (Courtesy Robert Hickox family.)

A 1930S PATROL WAGON. The wagon is stopped next to a signal service call box at Huntington Avenue and Hemenway Street. (Courtesy Boston Police Department Archives.)

A 1964 Ford Custom Cruiser. This *c.* 1968 photograph shows a cruiser that was in use at the time. (Courtesy Boston Herald.)

A Ford Crown Victoria Cruiser. A more modern police vehicle, the Ford Crown Victoria cruiser, is seen in this *c.* 2001 photograph. (Courtesy Boston Police Department Archives.)

BULLET-RESISTANT VESTS, C. 1964. These early vests were heavy and uncomfortable. The vests today are made from lightweight plastics and are nearly invisible under clothing. (Courtesy Boston Police Department Archives.)

A PATROL WAGON ANSWERING A CALL, C. 1886. In 1886, after approximately five years of trials at various divisions, all of the divisions were equipped with signal boxes by the Municipal Signal Company. These signal boxes allowed communication between patrol officers and the station houses. (Courtesy Boston Police Relief Association.)

A MOUNTED OFFICER. This officer is seen checking in with the station house in 1959. Signal boxes were in use until 1968. (Courtesy Boston Police Department Archives.)

A DEPARTMENT CHEMIST. The chemist seen here is testing a fluid that was found at the scene of a 1966 crime. The department's crime lab opened in 1960, and in 2002, it received accreditation from the Laboratory Accreditation Board of the American Society of Crime Laboratory Directors. (Courtesy Boston Police Department Archives.)

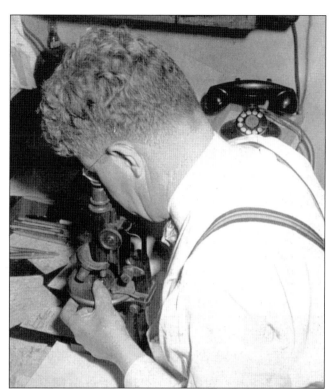

CHEMIST FRANK STRATTON.
Stratton is lending lab support
to a homicide investigation in
1959. (Courtesy Boston Police
Department Archives.)

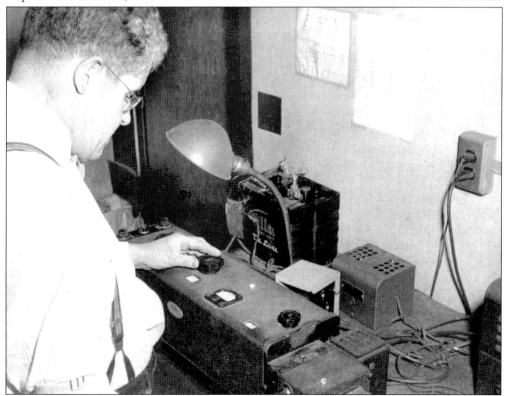

TESTING FOR LATENT PRINTS ON A STOLEN VEHICLE IN 1960. Fingerprints were not recognized as identifiers until the late 19th century, when Sir Francis Galton wrote a report on fingerprints. By the early 20th century, fingerprints as a means of identification were widely accepted in Europe and the United States. The new Galton system replaced the older Bertillon system, which had been based upon body measurements and characteristics. (Courtesy Boston Police Department Archives.)

A MOBILE LABORATORY. Seen here is the crime lab's mobile laboratory in 1994. (Courtesy Boston Police Department Archives.)

TEST FIRING A WEAPON. This weapon, used in a 1964 crime, was test fired for comparison purposes. The department's ballistics unit opened in 1935 and today has the most technologically advanced ballistics equipment in the Northeast, including an Integrated Ballistics Identification System (IBIS) with linkage to the Bureau of Alcohol, Tobacco, Firearms, and Explosives (ATF) gun-tracing center in Virginia. IBIS traces bullets and guns by identifying the marks left on bullets by a gun's barrel, firing pin, extractor, or breach block. (Courtesy Boston Police Department Archives.)

THE CAR AVAILABILITY BOARD IN 1966. It is difficult to believe that the complex function of dispatch was handled in such a fashion. In 1966, 504,448 emergency messages were received and processed at the central complaint desk. Also received were 254,493 teletype messages and 235 telegrams. A total of 2,104,935 radio messages were sent or received. (Courtesy Boston Police Department Archives.)

OPERATIONS IN THE "TURRET," c. THE 1970s. In 1972, the department installed the 911 system, necessitating a greater use of computers. In 1995, Enhanced 911, and a computer-aided dispatch system linked to mobile data terminals, was installed. This state-of-the-art system allows for priority sorting of emergency calls. (Courtesy Boston Herald.)

Four

THE 1919 BOSTON POLICE STRIKE

RESTORING ORDER AFTER THE STRIKE. These unidentified superior officers are in a Model T Ford with an air-cooled machine gun perched in the rear seat. Many volunteer officers were recruited for the crisis, including Harvard's football team. After several days of rioting, in which at least six people died, the Massachusetts State Guard was called in. (Courtesy Boston Police Department Archives.)

JOHN FRANKLIN MCINNES, C. 1919. McInnes was appointed in 1907 and served as the vice president of the Boston Social Club, the forerunner of the police union, for which he served as president. In September 1919, he was dismissed for forming the union along with 18 other union leaders. In response, over 1,100 of Boston's 1,500 officers went on strike. (Courtesy James Cregg.)

App. Nov. 10, 1898.

	Rank	Div.
Blue, Malcolm D.	Patrolman	1

Com. *p. 369, 435, Saved life.* *Saved life.*

ABANDONED HIS DUTY SEPTEMBER 9, 1919.

●

PATROLMAN BLUE'S ROSTER CARD. This card was stamped, "Abandoned His Duty September 9, 1919." Patrolman Blue's roster card, along with those of his 1,100 fellow officers, represent the very real price that early labor activists paid to gain the better working conditions and wages that are enjoyed by many today. (Courtesy Boston Police Department Archives.)

As Related to

HARRY McCORMICK, *Traveler* Police Reporter

No. 103—Patrolman Malcolm D. Blue

For many years Patrolman Malcolm D. Blue of the Hanover street station has done duty in the North end section. Naturally he has had encounters with thieves and other law breakers.

To his mind the thrill of thrills came in the rescue of a drowning man, in the early morning hours of a chill day in winter.

"I remember one mixup that was not only thrilling but came near being fatal for me," he said. "Two men had quarrelled on Travers street. One had shot the other and as I hastened to the spot the man that had done the shooting was running away. I followed after him and when I was about to close in on him he fired.

"The bullet went through my helmet. I got the man before he could fire again. The helmet I still preserve and every time I look at it I thank my lucky star.

"But this drowning rescue was my real thrill. I was doing night work and while patrolling a section near Lewis wharf heard a cry for help. Rushing to the side of the wharf I could make out the form of a man struggling in the water. I quickly removed my coat (it was in the winter time), club and gun and plunged into the icy waters after the man. A few strokes and I was at his side. As I tried to get a grip on him he reached out his hand and got a death grip on my throat. I tried to throw him off, but he clung on. To make matters worse he struggled furiously and I was beginning to feel the strain.

Patrolman Malcolm D. Blue.

a boat was put out. We got the man ashore and summoned an ambulance.

"He was pretty well used up, as he had hurt himself when he fell.

"And incidentally I was in bad shape

A *Boston Traveler* Newspaper Column. In 1916, the *Boston Traveler* ran a daily column entitled "My Most Thrilling Experience: Exciting Moments in the Lives of Boston Policemen." In the column for April 24, 1916, Patrolman Malcolm D. Blue was highlighted for rescuing a drowning man. (Courtesy Boston Police Department Archives.)

STATION 10, 1919. This station served as one of the centers from which the Massachusetts State Guardsmen operated. Police Capt. James Gallivan was in charge of the station and commanded the guard unit assigned to the territory. (Courtesy Boston Police Department Archives.)

STATION 9, 1919. Station 9 also served as a center for the guardsmen. Capt. Perley Skillings was the captain here, and Capt. Henry Crowell took charge of the guard unit assigned to duty here. (Courtesy Boston Police Department Archives.)

THE A COMPANY, 11TH REGIMENT, INFANTRY, MASSACHUSETTS STATE GUARD. Many units of the state guard responded to the call for assistance during the strike; among them were the 10th Regiment, the 11th Regiment, the 12th Regiment, the 14th Regiment, the 15th Regiment, the 20th Regiment, the 1st Cavalry Troop, the 1st Motor Corps, and the Ambulance Corps. This photograph was taken on October 25, 1919. (Courtesy Boston Police Department Archives.)

MASSACHUSETTS STATE GUARDSMEN WITH MOTORCYCLES, C. 1919. These officers were part of the contingent that was assigned to help restore order in Boston in the aftermath of the strike. (Courtesy Boston Police Department Archives.)

Five

SPECIALIZED UNITS

ON THE SET OF BOOMTOWN IN 1959. *Boomtown* was a much-loved Boston children's television show that ran from 1959 to 1974. The star of the show was Rex Trailer, who still lives in the Boston area and teaches classes in television performance and production at Emerson College. Seen here are unidentified members of the M-1 safety squad on the set of the show. (Courtesy Boston Police Department Archives.)

THE M-1 SAFETY SQUAD, C. THE 1950S. The squad is with schoolchildren in front of the Lyman School on Paris Street in East Boston. The Dante Alighieri School is in the background. (Courtesy Boston Police Department Archives.)

THE M-1 SAFETY SQUAD GIVES A PRESENTATION TO SCHOOLCHILDREN. As seen in this 1962 photograph, the squad presented safety programs to children at local schools. They also addressed industrial organizations, armed services, and civic clubs. The unit produced a weekly children's radio show every Sunday morning on WORL. (Courtesy Boston Police Department Archives.)

THE RIOT SQUAD. The Boston Police Department Riot Squad is seen in this *c.* 1924 photograph. (Courtesy Boston Herald.)

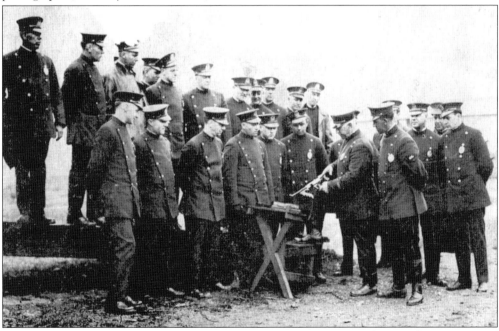

CAPT. LOUIS E. LUTZ WITH THE RIOT SQUAD. Captain Lutz is explaining the operation of the Thompson Submachine Gun to the squad at Fort Standish in Boston Harbor *c.* the early 1930s. (Courtesy Boston Police Relief Association.)

OFFICERS OF THE TACTICAL PATROL FORCE, C. THE 1970S. This unit was established in 1962 to provide a highly mobile foot patrol of officers to augment the officers of the districts and units when unusual or sudden emergencies occurred. They were utilized extensively in 1974, when court-ordered busing began in Boston. (Courtesy Boston Police Department Archives.)

K-9 Officers and a Dog on the Trail in 1964. This unit began with six dogs donated by German reporters grateful for the cooperation they had received from Boston officers in their coverage of the Boston Strangler murders. They also paid for the chief dog trainer of the Berlin Police Department to come to Boston for six months to teach Boston's officers how to work with the dogs. (Courtesy Boston Police Department Archives.)

The K-9 Unit. Seen here are officers of the unit with Donna, a police dog, in 1964. (Courtesy Boston Police Department Archives.)

UNIDENTIFIED MOBILE OFFICER ON A HARLEY-DAVIDSON WITH A SIDECAR, 1967. The Harley has been the motorcycle of choice for the department for more than 35 years. It does exude a certain presence. (Courtesy Boston Police Department Archives.)

INDIAN MOTORCYCLES. This *c.* 1920s photograph shows officers and their Indian motorcycles. (Courtesy Boston Police Department Archives.)

A 1920s Parade. Here, Boston policemen are on parade with motorcycle officers in the lead.(Courtesy Boston Police Department Archives.)

An Officer and His Motorcycle. This unidentified officer is seen *c.* 1967 with his Harley motorcycle. (Courtesy Boston Police Department Archives.)

UNIDENTIFIED MOUNTED OFFICER, C. THE EARLY 1920S. Mounted officers patrolled the more remote areas of their divisions, as can be seen by the rural character of this officer's surroundings. (Courtesy Boston Police Department Archives.)

A MOUNTED OFFICER, C. 1901. This unidentified mounted officer was from Division 11. (Courtesy Boston Police Department Archives.)

A MOUNTED OFFICER, C. 1906. The unidentified officer is on Henchman Street in the North End. (Courtesy Boston Police Department Archives.)

Boston Horse Show.
October 30, 1924.

OFFICERS ON PARADE. Unidentified mounted officers are seen in a *c.* 1929 parade. (Courtesy Boston Herald.)

MOUNTED OFFICERS. These unidentified officers are located in front of headquarters, at 154 Berkeley Street, *c.* the 1930s. (Courtesy Boston Herald.)

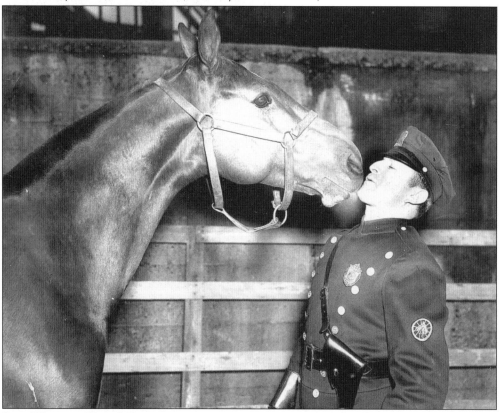

SGT. WILLIAM "PETE" DOOLEY AND A FRIEND, C. 1943. Sergeant Dooley was appointed in 1920 and served as the horse buyer for the department. He was also in charge of breaking and training the horses. (Courtesy Boston Herald.)

A MOUNTED OFFICER WITH JUNIOR POLICE RECRUITS, C. 1997. Junior Police Recruits is one of the many youth programs that the department sponsors. (Courtesy Boston Police Department Archives.)

THE GUARDIAN, C. 1901. In 1853, the Harbor Police was created in response to the increase in robberies of occupied vessels in the waters of Boston Harbor. The officers were furnished with rowboats and armed with Colt revolvers. This was the first unit furnished with firearms. (Courtesy Boston Police Department Archives.)

THE HARBOR PATROL. In this 1960 photograph, the Harbor Patrol retrieves the body of a boating-accident victim. (Courtesy Boston Police Department Archives.)

A 1966 RESCUE. Here, three boys are saved from a drifting raft by the Harbor Police. (Courtesy Boston Police Department Archives.)

THE VIGILANT. Another Harbor Police craft is seen in this 1967 photograph. (Courtesy Boston Police Department Archives.)

JUNIOR POLICE RECRUITS ON HARBOR PATROL. These young recruits are aboard the *Saint Michael* in 1997. (Courtesy Boston Police Department Archives.)

A Seized Drug Cache. Here, unidentified officers examine a drug cache seized after a long surveillance in 1963. (Courtesy Boston Police Department Archives.)

The Vice Squad. In this *c.* 1960s photograph, officers are seen examining materials seized in a raid. From left to right are Detectives Willis Saunders, Dennis Casey, Harry Manos, and Arthur "the Ferret" Linsky, so known because of his extraordinary ability to sniff out illegal drugs on raids. (Courtesy Boston Herald.)

MEMBERS OF THE DRUG SQUAD. This raid occurred in 1975. From left to right are Detectives Herb Spellman, Vinny Logan, George Costigan, and Tom Maher. (Courtesy Boston Herald.)

THE EXPLOSIVE ORDINANCE UNIT AT WORK IN 2001. The "Bomb Squad" was established in 1963 to address an increasing number of incidents involving explosives or other dangerous materials. In 1991, the unit lost Officer Jeremiah Hurley Jr. when he was called to the scene of a reported bomb. Hurley and Officer Francis Foley were handling the bomb when it exploded, killing Hurley and severely injuring Foley. (Courtesy Boston Police Department Archives.)

A Bicycle Officer in 1994. The tradition of Boston officers on bicycles goes back to 1896, when four park police were furnished with bicycles. (Courtesy Boston Police Department Archives.)

The Dive Team, a Unit of Special Operations. Among other duties, members of the dive team search for missing victims of swimming and boating accidents. This photograph was taken in 2001. (Courtesy Boston Police Department Archives.)

Six

FIGHTING CRIME AND SAVING LIVES

THE SCENE OF PATROLMAN JOHN GALLAGHER'S MURDER, MAY 25, 1962. The officer in the black raincoat is John J. Daley. The other officers are unidentified. The murder suspect was apprehended, and he served a life sentence. John Daley's two sons, John J. Daley Jr. and Richard G. Daley, joined the force and are sergeant detectives assigned to the gang unit and the District D-4 Drug Squad, respectively. (Courtesy Boston Herald.)

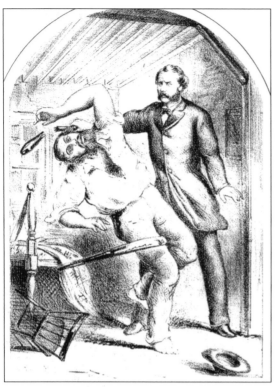

EDWARD SAVAGE AND JOHN WELCH. Here, Savage is seen defending himself against an attack by Welch. Savage arrested Welch in 1854. John Welch was convicted and sentenced to two years in the house of correction for cruelty to his wife. This image appears in Savage's 1873 book, *Police Recollections or Boston by Daylight and Gaslight*. (Author's collection.)

"RAT PITS," AN ILLUSTRATION FROM SAVAGE'S 1873 BOOK. Savage writes, "I never objected to the matter of destroying any quantity of rats, but the ceremonies attending these rat-pit exhibitions most surely tend to cultivate and nurse the evils, vices, and crime to which the proprietor of this pit fell a victim [he was stabbed to death]." Plus de choses changent le plus qu'ils restent la même chose; the more things change, the more they stay the same. (Author's collection.)

PICKPOCKETS. Seen is another illustration from Savage's book, in which he writes, "Some officers seem to think it prudent to give notice when a pickpocket is seen in a crowd, and immediately cry out 'Pickpockets, look out for your wallets!' . . . but this is the very thing he should not do, for no sooner comes such word of caution than every man's hand almost involuntarily goes to his wallet, [revealing all] to the wily thief." (Author's collection.)

THOMAS DAVIE, SAFE BLOWER, C. 1887. This is one of the thousands of criminal identification cards maintained in the "Rogues' Gallery" in the 19th and early 20th centuries. On the back of each card was listed all of the information known about each individual, such as physical characteristics, modus operandi, known associates, and any warrants issued. (Courtesy Boston Police Department Archives.)

Wanted for Murder of Josephine Brown,
ON DECEMBER 24th, 1891.

ROGER T. SCANNEL al. R. O'CONNELL,

Twenty-six (26) years of age; five (5) feet eight (8) inches in height; one hundred and forty (140) to one hundred and forty-five (145) pounds weight; complexion medium but inclined to light; small light-colored mustache; high cheek bones; face narrowing sharply from cheek bones to chin; consumptive look; pretty square shoulders viewed from behind; small waist and hips; one shoulder a little lower than the other; first joint of forefinger on left hand a little out and turned in on account of an accident.

Wore at that time a flat-topped Scotch Cap with two or three buttons in front; blue and white Gingham Shirt; black cutaway Coat and Vest; blue and black stripes in Pants, and a Gray Check Ulster, brown stripe, well worn, four pockets on the outside and one in each sleeve.

Speaks with a slight brogue and an affected air; wears a 14 1-2 Collar and No. 8 or No. 9 Shoe. Frequents kitchen bar-rooms and cheap lodging rooms with low women.

FAC-SIMILE OF HANDWRITING:

AN 1891 WANTED POSTER. This illustration is from the 1897 Watt and Eldridge book, *Our Rival, the Rascal—A Faithful Portrayal of the Conflict Between the Criminals of this Age and the Defenders of Society—The Police.* This is a sample of the many wanted posters issued by the superintendent's office in the 19th century. (Author's collection.)

ROSIE YOKAR.   ROSIE COHEN.

A SHOPLIFTING GANG, C. 1897. With another illustration from the Watt and Eldridge book, the authors write, "When this gang was arrested, fully fifteen hundred dollars worth of fine silks and other costly cloth were found in trunks in their rooms and there was good reason for holding that the women's contribution to this stock was fully as large as that made by the men." (Author's collection.)

BRINK'S CASHIER THOMAS B. LLOYD AND BRINK'S GUARD JAMES C. ALLEN. Here, Lloyd appears in the foreground. In 1950, a gang of 11 men planned and executed a nearly perfect crime. They stole $2,775,395.12 in cash, checks, and money orders from Brink's. They were apprehended in 1956, 11 days before the state statute would have run out. Lloyd and Allen are recreating the positions that the robbers made them take. (Courtesy Boston Police Department Archives.)

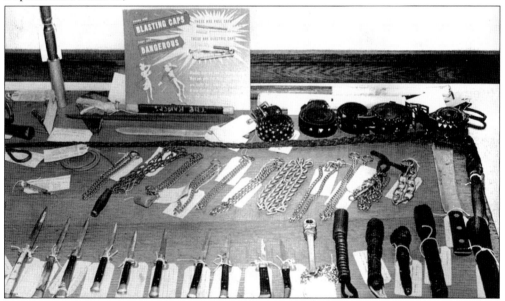

A TEENAGE ARSENAL. This picture was printed in the 1958 Boston Police Department annual report. That year, juvenile officers arrested 2,321 male and 428 female juveniles between the ages of 7 and 16. (Courtesy Boston Police Department Archives.)

A Traffic Stop, c. the 1970s. According to the Uniform Crime Report, issued by the Federal Bureau of Investigation, approximately 15 percent of police officer line-of-duty deaths between 1992 and 2001 resulted from traffic stops gone bad. (Courtesy Boston Herald.)

OFFICERS JACK SULLIVAN AND RICHIE DOYLE OF DIVISION 4 IN 1981. Officer Sullivan was appointed in 1970 and retired as a deputy superintendent in 2001. Officer Richie Doyle was appointed in 1966 and retired as a sergeant detective in 2003. (Courtesy Boston Herald.)

OFFICER JACK SULLIVAN HANDCUFFS A MUGGING SUSPECT IN 1981. Sullivan's partner, Officer Richie Doyle, looks on. The hatchet the suspect allegedly used in the crime lies on the hood of the patrol car. (Courtesy Boston Herald.)

A COMBINED RAID IN ROXBURY AND DORCHESTER. The Boston Police Department Burglary Task Force and the federal Drug Enforcement Administration teamed up in a 1982 raid in Roxbury and Dorchester. (Courtesy Boston Herald.)

A MURDER SUSPECT ARRESTED IN 1981. Homicide officers Sgt. Det. Stephen Murphy and Det. Paul Murphy lead Wendall Burton, the suspected killer of Back Bay nurse Deborah Smith, into headquarters at 154 Berkeley Street. (Courtesy Boston Herald.)

A 1994 CRIME SCENE. Then Superintendent in Chief Paul Evans, Det. Eddie McNelly, Det. Herbert Spellman, and Det. Charlie Horsely (from left to right) are at the scene of the death of Eric Sheppard in Dorchester. The boy, age 7, had killed himself with an abandoned gun he had found. (Courtesy Boston Herald.)

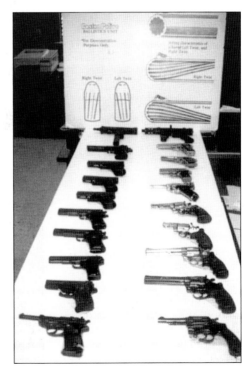

WEAPONS CONFISCATED BY THE BALLISTICS UNIT IN 1994. The unit destroyed nearly 1,900 confiscated weapons in 1994. (Courtesy Boston Police Department Archives.)

SGT. DET. TOM O'LEARY. O'Leary, a homicide detective, gathers evidence in a 1996 homicide case. (Courtesy Boston Police Department Archives.)

THE OPEN-WINDOW APPROACH TO PATROL. Neighborhood policing is seen in action in 1994. (Courtesy Boston Police Department Archives.)

BOSTON OFFICIALS IN 1872.
Mayor William Gaston, Police
Chief Edward Savage, and
Fire Chief John S. Damrell
were in office when fire swept
across Boston in November
1872. Boston's officers
arrested hundreds of looters
and recovered approximately
$400,000 worth of property.
There was so much drunkenness
the next day that Chief Savage
closed all of the bars and
forbade any sales of beer and
liquor until the crisis was over.
(Author's collection.)

BOSTON IN FLAMES. The Boston Police Relief Association was started by a donation of $500 from Chicago's chief of police, Elmer Washburne, after the fire. It was accompanied by a letter to Chief Savage, which read, "For the Boys, B.P." (Author's collection.)

"NOCTURNAL STROLL COMES CROPPER AS OFFICER TAKES OVER IN CHARLESTOWN." This photograph, showing an unidentified Boston officer assisting a lost child, was included in the 1961 Boston Police Department annual report with the above title. (Courtesy Boston Police Department Archives.)

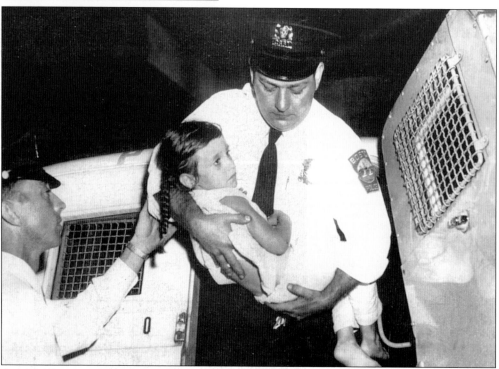

A 1961 RESCUE. Here, an unidentified Boston officer carries a young fire victim into Boston City Hospital. (Courtesy Boston Police Department Archives.)

AIDING A FIREFIGHTER. In this 1961 photograph, unidentified Boston officers and a firefighter aid a disabled firefighter. (Courtesy Boston Police Department Archives.)

UNIDENTIFIED BOSTON OFFICER AIDING AN UNIDENTIFIED VICTIM, C. THE 1960S–1970S. Boston's police officers are often the first on the scene after violent acts and do not hesitate to offer first aid. (Courtesy Boston Herald.)

A 1964 House Fire. An unidentified Boston officer kicks in a window of a house in flames. (Courtesy Boston Police Department Archives.)

A Rescued Toddler. This patrolman shows his joy after the 1964 rescue of a toddler. (Courtesy Boston Police Department Archives.)

Seven

MISCELLANY

OFFICERS OF DIVISION 10, C. THE 1870S. The Division 10 station at 1170 Columbus Avenue at Roxbury Crossing was occupied from 1869 until 1971. (Courtesy Boston Police Department Archives.)

DIVISION 10, A C. 1877 VIEW. Seen are the officers of Division 10 at 1170 Columbus Avenue at Roxbury Crossing. (Courtesy Boston Police Department Archives.)

OFFICERS OF STATION 1, THE OLD HANCOCK SCHOOL, AFTER 1881. This building, located at 209 Hanover Street, was in use for Night Watch and police purposes from 1849 until 1933, when the division moved to new premises at 154 North Street. (Courtesy Boston Police Department Archives.)

OFFICERS OF STATION 11, KANE SQUARE, AFTER 1881. Established with the annexation of Dorchester in 1870, the district remained at this location in Neponset-Dorchester until 1875. (Courtesy Boston Police Department Archives.)

THE "MILITARY MARCH AND TWO STEP." Seen here is a cover sheet for the song that was dedicated to the Boston Police Department in 1901. The march was played for the first time at an annual ball of the Boston Police Relief Association in 1900 or 1901. The music was declared to be the "official musical number of the police," and was to be "played on all occasions wherein the force takes part." The composer, George Goodwin, was an electrician in the department's Signal Corps. (Author's collection.)

DEPARTMENT ATHLETES. The Division 9 baseball team is seen in this *c.* 1929 photograph. (Courtesy Boston Police Department Archives.)

THE BOSTON POLICE ON PARADE, OCTOBER 12, 1922. This parade included all of the command staff, all of the division captains, the Y.D. Veterans Band, the 110 Cavalry, M.N.G. Band, the Boston Police Traffic Division Band, four mounted men from the traffic division as skirmishers, the sergeant and 20 mounted men from Division 16, six patrolmen (each carrying a Thompson Submachine Gun), the motorcycle unit, a unit of vehicles with mounted machine

guns, patrol wagons from Divisions 13 and 14, and two mounted men from Division 20 to ride at the rear of the parade. The superintendent of police, Michael H. Crowley, commanded that "every officer in the Department, who is not sick, will take part in the parade, go on street duty on his Division, or will hold himself in readiness in his station house until after the parade is over." (Courtesy Boston Police Detectives Benevolent Society.)

DIVISION 10. This photograph of the 1170 Columbus Avenue station of Division 10 was taken *c.* the 1920s. (Courtesy Boston Police Relief Association.)

CHARLES S. GRELL AND THOMAS B. LLOYD. Seen here are Grell, a Brink's guard, on the left, and Lloyd, a Brink's cashier, on the right, in 1950. Grell is crouching at the side of one of the carts that the robbers used to transport the loot to their truck. (Courtesy Boston Police Department Archives.)

RESTRAINING A PRISONER. In this 1960 photograph, unidentified Boston officers restrain an unruly prisoner. (Courtesy Boston Police Department Archives.)

MOUNTED OFFICERS ON TRAFFIC DUTY IN 1958. These officers are at the intersection of Washington and Summer Streets, Boston's busiest intersection in 1958. (Courtesy Boston Police Department Archives.)

TRAFFIC DUTY. This unidentified Boston officer is on duty in 1958 in a traffic box. (Courtesy Boston Police Department Archives.)

THE WALTER SCOTT MEDAL FOR VALOR.
In 1922, Walter Scott donated $2,000 to
the city government to create a fund for
the purpose of honoring the firefighter or
police officer who, in the judgment of his
commissioner, had "especially distinguished
himself for valor." (Courtesy Boston Police
Department Archives.)

**THE DEPARTMENTAL MEDAL OF
HONOR.** The medal was established
by an act of the city council on
February 7, 1898, for any member
cited for extraordinary courage or
bravery. (Courtesy Boston Police
Department Archives.)

NEW EQUIPMENT. Seen here are new patrol wagons in 1959. (Courtesy Boston Police Department Archives.)

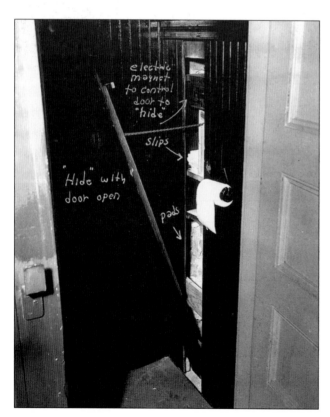

A BOOKIE'S HIDE. A bookie's hide in a bookie joint was discovered at 2420 Washington Street in Roxbury, c. the 1960s. (Courtesy Boston Police Department Archives.)

NO MATTER WHAT THE WEATHER. An unidentified Boston police officer directs traffic in 1959. (Courtesy Boston Police Department Archives.)

"MURDER IN THE SHADOWS." This photograph was printed in the 1959 Boston Police Department annual report. (Courtesy Boston Herald.)

PRESIDENT-ELECT KENNEDY RETURNS TO BOSTON IN 1960. John F. Kennedy is surrounded by a guard of Boston's police officers. (Courtesy Boston Police Department Archives.)

A TRIUMPHANT PARADE FOR JOHN F. KENNEDY IN 1961. Kennedy is escorted by mounted, motorcycle, and foot officers. (Courtesy Boston Police Department Archives.)

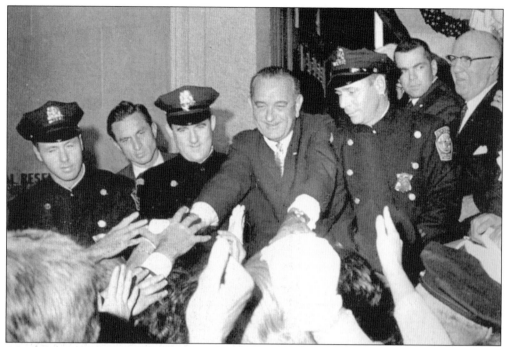

ANOTHER PRESIDENTIAL VISIT. President Johnson is seen in Boston in 1964. (Courtesy Boston Police Department Archives.)

PRESIDENT CLINTON MEETS WITH DEPARTMENT OFFICIALS. President Clinton is seen with Commissioner Paul Evans and Patrolman Thomas Nee, the president of the Boston Police Patrolmen's Association. This photograph was taken in 1997. (Courtesy Boston Police Department Archives.)

A 1959 PRISONER. This unidentified officer escorts a prisoner into a cell in 1959. (Courtesy Boston Police Department Archives.)

A LOST TODDLER. An unidentified officer is seen with a lost Charlestown toddler in 1960. (Courtesy Boston Police Department Archives.)

ON PARADE. Seen here is the Boston Police Department Band on parade *c.* 1960. (Courtesy Boston Herald.)

THE JOHN GALLAGHER SHOOTING. This photograph shows the scene outside of the National Shawmut Bank after John Gallagher was shot on May 25, 1962. Patrolman Gallagher was killed while attempting to apprehend a suspect who was committing a bank burglary. (Courtesy Boston Herald.)

COMMISSIONER LEO SULLIVAN WITH JIMMY DURANTE, C. 1960. Here, the commissioner is pinning a miniature badge on Jimmy Durante, who had donated his time to the Jimmy Fund in cooperation with the department. (Courtesy Boston Herald.)

JIMMY DURANTE. Durante is at Commissioner Sullivan's desk, showing off his new badge. (Courtesy Boston Herald.)

BOSTON POLICE ACADEMY CLASS, JUNE 4, 1952. Individual officers have not been identified, but according to department records, the following officers were appointed on June 4, 1952: Arthur Blinn, Paul Bouzane, Gerald Bulman, Vincent Clifford, Leo Corbett, Richard Crowley, James Donadini, Timothy Donovan, Mario Ferro, Francis Hanrahan, John Madden, Richard McLeod, Peter Mortimer, Francis Nazzaro, Gerald Ridge, John Ryan Jr., and Norman Spellberg. (Courtesy Boston Police Department Archives.)

TAKING A BREAK. Here, a group of Boston officers take a break *c.* the 1980s. (Courtesy Boston Herald.)

"GREETINGS FROM THE BOSTON POLICE DEPARTMENT," 1996. The Boston Police Department marches in a parade in 1996. (Courtesy Boston Police Department Archives.)

THE ROLL OF HONOR

Jonathan Houghton   Died December 11, 1825
David Estes   Died April 27, 1848
Ezekial W. Hodsdon   Died October 17, 1857
Alfred M. Sturdivant   Died September 4, 1904
John T. Lynch   Died January 16, 1908
Frederick Schlehuber   Died November 10, 1910
Richard J. Gallivan   Died February 8, 1911
Albert R. Peterson   Died October 29, 1912
Thomas J. Norton   Died June 19, 1914
Patrick J. Carr   Died August 1, 1916
John J. Earle   Died October 20, 1916
Joseph C. Reiser   Died January 20, 1918
Charles E. Deininger   Died February 13, 1919
Adolph F. Butterman   Died June 16, 1919
William G. Clancy   Died January 22, 1920
Ward M. Bray   Died April 14, 1921
Andrew B. Cuneo   Died August 13, 1921
Daniel J. McShane   Died January 31, 1922
Peter P. Oginskis   Died May 5, 1923
Joseph E. Gonya   Died October 21, 1923
Albert Motroni   Died September 22, 1924
Benjamin Alexander   Died July 4, 1925
Frank J. Comeau   Died March 24, 1926
Harris B. McInnes   Died July 3, 1927
Herbert D. Allen   Died December 25, 1927
Edward Q. Butters   Died August 14, 1929
John I. Jackson   Died September 4, 1929
James J. Troy   Died January 13, 1930
Franklin B. Dreyer   Died April 24, 1930
Frederick W. Bartlett   Died December 10, 1930
Joseph L. Cavagnaro   Died November 17, 1931
William L. Abbot   Died November 28, 1931
John P. M. Wolfe   Died December 1, 1931
George J. Hanley   Died March 20, 1934
James T. Malloy   Died June 4, 1934
James Brickley   Died November 25, 1934
Daniel A. McCallum   Died May 12, 1935
James D. Hughes   Died September 10, 1935
James B. Roche   Died March 21, 1936
James G. McCann Jr.   Died June 16, 1937
Laurence V. Sheridan   Died July 28, 1937
Walter Baxter   Died August 4, 1937
Edward J. Kelley   Died January 14, 1938
John H. Manning   Died February 6, 1938
Paul J. Murnane   Died September 23,1938
Thomas A. Davis   Died April 13, 1939
Patrick C. Gannon   Died April 2, 1940

Stephan P. Harrigan   Died January 7, 1941
Frank B. Callahan   Died February 20, 1945
William F. Healey   Died October 2, 1946
Michael J. Crowley   Died May 12, 1961
John J. Gallagher   Died May 25, 1962
James B. O'Leary   Died August 2, 1963
George J. Holmes   Died November 6, 1963
Charles A. McNabb   Died November 23, 1968
Francis B. Johnson   Died March 17, 1969
John D. Schroeder   Died September 24, 1970
Joseph M. Mullen   Died December 18, 1972
Walter A. Schroeder   Died November 30, 1973
Donald A. Brown   Died May 24, 1974
Francis E. Creamer   Died October 7, 1974
Richard F. Halloran   Died November 6, 1975
William R. Beckman   Died September 1, 1976
Roy J. Sergei   Died October26, 1987
Thomas J. Gill   Died February 10, 1988
Sherman C. Griffiths   Died February 17, 1988
Louis H. Metaxas   Died August 27, 1989
Jeremiah J. Hurley Jr.   Died October 28, 1991
Thomas F. Rose   Died February 18, 1993
John J. Mulligan   Died September 26, 1993
B. Wayne Anderson   Died February 5, 1994

A 1960 MEMORIAL. Seen here is a gun volley commemorating Boston's fallen officers in 1960. (Courtesy Boston Police Department Archives.)

NEW HEADQUARTERS, ONE SCHROEDER PLAZA. Family members of fallen officers participate in the dedication of One Schroeder Plaza on June 17, 1998. (Courtesy Carla Osberg.)